The Eyes of Love

Poems by

Raymond Souster

A NOTE FROM THE AUTHOR

A few words concerning this book may be in order.
The first part, entitled "From a Young Man in Love,"
consists of poems I wrote and gave to my wife
in 1946 and 1947,
just before and just after our marriage.
The second part, entitled "Sequence for Susi,"
was written to commemorate the proud milestone
of our forty years of married life,
with all the turmoil and joy that went with them.
The mood of the poems is one of celebration.
Here then are the words of a young man
and those of that same man forty years later,
a little wiser, perhaps, if worn and sometimes shaken
by four decades of living.
If his later poems are the sadder for the passing
of time, they still sing of the same love
and the same joy.
For me this is enough.

This book is for Rosalia, my Susi, who was the inspiration for the poems and simply by being herself gave them whatever life they may possess.

From a Young Man in Love

1946-1947

YOU

You are my happy summer, my flaring rocket
Soaring into a sky now darkening,
And lighting up our grey impenetrable city
With the colours of your lips, your hair, your eyes.

O you are my carnival, my Sunnyside
Of roller-coasters, popcorn, nervous lights,
You are the solitary tree outside my window
Shining with warmth and rain, erect and proud,
Tossing her head into the morning wind.

KITTEN

O my little kitten, my soft beautiful lovely,
When you came into my life the long, empty hours
Became like forgotten dreams in a child's nightmare;
The world widened, the sky parted,
And all the angels of joy touched me with their wings.

But if you should leave me I know I should walk
Alone in an endless blackout through this cold city,
Looking at no face, letting no thought burn my brain,
And feeling everywhere on me the mocking laughter of a
    thousand eyes.

GOLDEN SUMMER

This is our golden summer,
It is ours alone,
Not ours to share
Nor to be taken from us.

Darling, reach up and squeeze the sun
In your joyous hands,
Kiss the blue water
With your lips' laughter.

It is said there is death
And darkness in our city;
But I am tired of the smell of death
And his dark pimp of night.

So when you take my hand and say,
Let us sit in the grass,
There are only the two of us living
In the golden summer of our love.

7

NIAGARA

You are like this river called Niagara,
With your beauty soft and soothing
As its banks, with your moods like this water,
Flowing peacefully, still as dusk, or wild
As its seething whirlpools, sudden dangerous eddies;

You glide as easily, as perfectly
Into my life as the green smoothness of Niagara
Blends and becomes our blue Ontario.

ANOTHER MYSTERY

O how could such a frail creature
Capture me with a look
From her girlish eyes, and twist
On the rack of her body my own
In the lock of love?

O how could such a frail creature
Give me these sleepless nights
When I could cry out in pain?
Perhaps I shall never know—
Even want it so.

THE BEASTS

Here in the dark shadow of your verandah
We take those long, hard kisses that make us gasp
And suck in the night air like animals pursued
When we draw apart; and my hands meet your body
Under the coat, at first tenderly, translating its contours
Fingers to palm to head, and then roughly, hurting you,
Almost as if despising your breasts and your thighs,
All your body so close to my will and yet so far:
Your body mine and yet not mine.
                                So all our greatest desires,
Our hopes dwarfing the heavens, all wither and die
Before the gods of circumstance, cruel, bloodless beasts
Of our lives, of our time, grinning, death-breathing monsters.

ROSE IN YOUR HAIR

Perhaps you wonder how I could be so jealous
Of a flower, and, as it turned out later,
Not even a real one, only a clever trick of a rose.

But there it was resting
In the dark nest of your long, glistening hair,
And I was jealous of a flower, a paper flower,
That it should share the soft deep pillow of your beauty
With the rough head that was mine falling,
Sinking through depths like silk to peace like heaven.

9

IN THE SUN

The heat that is in us both, darling,
At this moment of lying together
Under a blue umbrella sky,

Is more than desire, more than loneliness gone forever,
Is the heat of all our endless, brimming summers
Awakening in our bodies, slow and hesitant now,

As wonderful to feel as the warm June sun above
Passionately, persistently probing our tingling bodies.

THE WORLD WAS ALL CRAZY

The world was all crazy yesterday.
From a streetcar I looked on the Sunday-morning city world
Of dark stores, darker streets and the first crowds
Of people coming from church or hunger-roused from their
    beds,
Heading for restaurants and food and coffee. And not one
    face I saw
Seemed to radiate light, not one shone with a deeper beauty
Born of inner truth or deep joy, all seemed to suck at the
    darkness
Like lost, blind souls. And O, all the world was lost, lost
    utterly,

Until I came to see you in the afternoon,
And our bodies folded together in a throbbing greeting,
Our lips met at the edge of give and take
And gave, took warmly. Then the dark world was suddenly
    bathed
In light and all its people
Seemed to lose their black masks, each face glowed
With the saving crystal light of gladness,
And the world was once again a great, familiar place
With you and I the only two people in it: O this our world
Shining for us, killing for us, gay for us, sad for us, still some-
    how wonderful.

THE SMALL JOYS

O darling, since I have known you,
My eyes have been opened in wonder
To the small joys of our loving:

The way we hold hands, the kiss after the last kiss,
Jokes always ending at the navel, the office scandals,
Late cups of coffee, just watching you brush the black
Swooning net that is your hair stroke after electric stroke.

Such things as these, which the world would laugh at,
Grown far too clever, far too distant from joy,
Are to you and me the binding certainties of our love,
The gold and silver of our nights and days.

THE PILLOW

It could only have happened between sleep
And that half-awareness born of desire
That comes deep in the night.

O I was tightly in your arms,
Your skin's rub soft and unbearable,
Like down to stroke the white flower of your neck,
And pressing you closer, more hungrily . . .

Then I was suddenly awake, and the pillow
Mocked me, emphasized the certain lack
Of you with me in these other hours
Of waiting somehow for day to come and you
Before me again, your dark head with its brown eyes,
Your body with its thousand dreams of music,
Your hands' touch like peace and promise after war.

"WHEN YOUR DARK HEAD
IS SUDDENLY BURIED"

When your dark head is suddenly buried
In my arms, and your face nuzzles there
Like a wild, frightened thing
Hiding from a world eager to kill or destroy—

Then that wild charging river that is my love
Becomes a stream heavy with gentleness,
Whose rippling fingers soothe and lull away
All else but peace and the sleek cat of love.

THE BENCH ON THE SIDE OF THE HILL

We found it quite by chance,
The bench on the side of the hill.
There it was, half-way down,
Crooked between two slender trees,
And suddenly we had lost
Our curiosity or whatever it was
To carry us farther, so we stayed there
Till the sun had lost us
And the night was cold,
With only our mouths really warm
In a place very silent and dark

With somehow singing shouting through my head.

THE HARP

My body is a harp and you are playing
Melodies over it night and day, which rise at times
To the great crescendo of blaring trumpets,
And at times is the single melancholy of a lute
Piped so purely and thinly. But always there is music
Flowing and ebbing through my echoing frame,
Always there is the touch of your hands
To keep me warm and vibrant in all my strings.

"O WHY CAN'T ALL THE WORLD"

O why can't all the world
Move toward its golden centre as we move
Closer and closer to our dream of love?

And people having all the beautiful bodies given them,
How is it they have any time left to cheat and kill
In any name, in any cause righteous or evil,
When it is summer and the nights are long,
And all the air shaken with the silver of little bells?

ESCAPE

This golden afternoon
Our feet tug at all the roads, our noses sniff all the clover,
Our arms and legs glow with the touch of the sun,
Our eyes are fed on browns and greens and blues
That are the grain, the meadow-grass, the sky.

All under the boundless heavens today are spread
These riches not to be measured by money, flesh of women,
    rule of power,
And you and I, walking hand-in-hand on this dusty country
    road,
Forget the city behind us, city with its smoke, its dirt and evil,
And for an hour or two slip loose of the loathsome chains
Tied to our hands, to our bodies, something always seeking
To clutch that star of hope still burning so distantly
Yet so brightly now in our twin-stirred hearts.

YOUR EYES, YOUR WORDS

Your eyes eat into my stomach,
Pierce me like a spear to my very bowels.
I am as one who lies on a battlefield
And gropes but cannot find his wound.

Your words are food to my lips,
Good grain, luscious fruit; or they can lash
With the cut of twenty whips one after another,
These words that ease themselves from your kiss-aching
    throat.

IN THE DARKNESS

Coming home last night how the dark folded us
And blinded us, how lost all our efforts
To climb from the valley, with trees standing mute
And ghostlike, and always the river running somewhere
Unseen with its even roar. Only the white ribbon of the path
Gave us any hope and led our feet—but then I had your hand
Warm and soft in mine—and so it wasn't dark, I could never
    be lost,
Feeling the pulse of your blood beating with my blood,
Feeling the flow of your love like a searchlight probing
The darkness of a sky heavy with the beat
Of tired wings. O strong piercing flash of your love!

SHY ONE, CAUTIOUS ONE

I want to wound your white throat,
I want to cover it with the purple bruises
Of my lips, lance it through and through
With the wild tiger of my love.

Shy one, cautious one,
This is no time for shyness,
No year for any caution,

From your slim waist to your thighs
Curving like waterfalls I read there
Poems more wonderful than starlight
Or moonlight bloodied by no war or the hate of men.

17

KEW BEACH

We feel away from the city, even though the downtown skyline
Blinks in the scarlet west, the day-dying west.
Grass under our feet like the softest
Deepest carpets, leaf-rustle overhead;
And the crowd walking silently in pairs,
Their feet softly tapping the rotting, well worn boardwalk.

Hold me close. Kiss me.
Feel the first lake breezes on your forehead
Like a benediction. Give me your lips again,
Melting in like the cupped petals of flowers.

And for one evening there is nothing but this peace,
No bitterness tearing at our hearts, no clumsy knives
To draw and to stab, tearing the clean whole flesh
Of our love. No sounds of the war
That they slide into slowly reaching our ears
(They prepare quietly, stealthily) : while the path
Of the rippling monlight reaching on up to heaven
Seems to invite us, seems to almost beckon,
So that we stand, its sparkle lighting our eyes,
Fanning the smouldering fires of the moon.

18

"I HAVE SEEN SUCH SUNLIGHT"

I have seen such sunlight shining from your eyes
As never glinted from any green leaf of my knowing,
And cheek to your cheek have rubbed against such fire
No open hearth could flare against the night.

Have watched a darkness greater than any evil
Of great bombs falling shadow your delicate face,
Have felt the smarting salt within your tears,
And started up in my sleep remembering your pain.

THE LONG YEAR OF A WEEK

It was the long year of a week, wasn't it, darling,
That your lips were stranger to me, and I sought
The cool slopes of your neck with my kisses to tell you
What was surging up like a great storm in my heart.

Then last night so thankfully I almost shyly
Lowered my lips to yours, touching them at first as gently
As I would your breasts or your thighs—
Then, when I felt your lips tightening, growing firmer,
Gently pressing mine, I answered them
More boldly, almost savagely, with my own;

And in that moment those seven days of patient waiting
Had faded into the mist of the past, and nothing mattered
But this now, our wealth of now linked with our rich forever.

"WHEN I AM NEAR YOU"

When I am near you there is nothing in my world
But your eyes, your lips, your body (whitest flower
From earth's hidden garden), and I am putty
In your hands, my strength bent to your slightest whim;
As simple a thing as your hand brushed against my arm
Can send me up in smoke.

O dark-haired wonder of my life,
When you are away the single candle of my nights
Flickers and dies to a wind that blows like death,
But is colder, sharper as it strikes my heart.

WITH MY LIPS

With my lips on the warm milk smoothness
Of your neck I drink long and hard
Of that limitless strength that I take
From your slender body.

O as a little child
Cries for the ripe breasts of his mother,
So my arms reach out for you,
To crush you with my need, wave upon wave.

ONE DAY

One day you will die
As I will die, as the good and beautiful die,
As the old man in rags and broken shoes walking up Bay Street
Not with a bundle of cardboard on his back,
But all the weight of our wasteful, purposeless lives, will die.

Those lips will be silent, will not breathe my name
Turning in sleep or desire, those limbs will be motionless
That touched my limbs so warmly, so softly, those hands
Folded forever, not woven in mine, not making
Those quick, impulsive gestures that I love.

O may I lie beside you on that day!

WITH YOU AWAY

Of course I try not to think of you, to blot out completely
The picture of you, or rather the many, many pictures
That my mind summons up on its screen at the slightest
    thought of your name,

But there's no use fooling anyone, least of all myself,
That I can by any effort great or small erase your memory
    like a brush
Rubbed over the scrawls on a blackboard, or lock you away
In some far-off, disused storeroom of my brain:

For you are the part of me that waits for the sun
To shine down on all the world, you are the stars'
Tenderness at evening glowing through my soul
With a high, steadfast flame. And here beside me
Or far from this place that has suddenly grown dead
Like a cemetery's darkest corner, you breathe life back
    into my blood,
And all the fruits of my hands seem too poor to lay at your feet.

"O YOUR LOOK IS SO YOUNG"

O your look is so young, so innocent,
How could I know you'd be
The subtle cord around my throat?

O with your delicate lips, your body
So slight, how could I know those lips
Would split my heart, that body touch like a flame
My tinder-quick desire?

O how was I to know
What I know now so well?

END OF A HOLIDAY

We sit on the bed,
And it is enough
That I look at you and you look at me,
And if there is anything said
It is really not needed at all.

Hello, darling, my eyes say to you,
Hello, darling, your eyes sparkle back,
And we have never been apart, no, never,
It has always been like this,
Me looking at you, you looking at me
Through months that seem rich as the longest years.

23

CRAZY SUNDAY

This is an explanation that does not explain
Anything or everything I said or did
All that long yesterday of tormenting you.
For how can you explain
Why love turns to hate and hate turns back to love
All in a minute or an hour or a day?

Now all there is to do
Is to blot out yesterday like an evil dream
(And it was) that shall leave no scar, no terror anywhere,
And run headlong into the sunshine of our future
With our love stronger, more certain, from knowing this
    moment's darkness.

RED FRUIT

From lying there on the bed like a slumbering cat
You turn at my coming like the petals opening on a flower,
And sinking down to your warmth of face and arms and hands,
I encounter your lips, red fruit which I recklessly devour.

A CLOUD

A dark, dark cloud goes across the sun,
And for an instant that cloud becomes a blackness
On all the world, matchng the sad world's darkness.

My anger is that cloud, that darkness falling
Across the green shining world of you and me,
But then is suddenly gone, has passed over,
And happy as a little child I run to your loving arms.

TRUCE

Darling, I am tired of fighting,
I am tired of feeling the arrows of your anger
Bury themselves in my flesh, tired of aiming
My stupid, cruel-edged spears at your smarting body.

Instead I would turn all my strength to your sleeping breasts,
Melt all my hate on the cauldron of your thighs.
And you, you with only love on your lips
Bring me to sweet crucifixion at your cross.

LIPS

Night is the coming of your lips to mine,
Those smooth, cool islands where my journeys cease
In wide-eyed, dreamy wonder. O I have known them
Pouting and cold, and only half-alive,
And nothing seemed to waken them. And I have known them
Reckless and burning, paining in their deep
Soul-rocking reach. That these lips could belong
To such a child's face, open with innocence,
Is something without reason. But who am I
To consider reason—when those lips wait to lock with mine?

TELEPHONE

Waiting to hear the phone ring,
Waiting to hear the sound of you
Across distance and time again.
God, how slow minutes can be,
Aching suspensions of living,
Moments of death, of darkness . . . .

Then the telephone jangles, my heart jumps
Into my mouth at the simple thought of you,
Talking to you, just revelling in your voice:

And suddenly, all through the house a brightness
Shining, glowing to match my quickened heartbeats!

26

LIKE THE PUNCH-DRUNK FIGHTER

I can fight all the world, O all of it,
Smashed by it, go back for more
Like the punch-drunk fighter with the iron head
Always getting up on the count of nine;

But you must be beside me, the touch
Of your hand held in mine, warmly, lovingly,
You must be there to take me in your arms
When I return with the good red blood of defeat
Or the green palm of victory in my careless hands.

CONSPIRACY

What reason makes your lips, breasts, arms, even thighs
    conspire
To fill me with such elemental fire?
Fire that leaps and flames and only dies
When it has seared and burned those lips, breasts, arms and
    thighs.

27

THERE WAS THUNDER IN THE NIGHT

There was thunder in the night and I woke this morning
To find it still with me, shaking up the sky,
And with it grey rain, the too-grey rain.

Litter of golden leaves on all the grass.

O I want your body to turn to, your breasts to hold,
To fondle, the warmth of your breathing to melt
This cold curse of autumn I woke to this morning
And deep in me now, thrusting its icy roots
Close to my heart. O God I want you,
You I home to like a storm-tossed bird
Beaten and heavy in his tireless wings.

"WHEN MY MIND IS NOT SOMEWHERE"

When my mind is not somewhere
Between the green meadow beginning at your breasts
And running to the shy well of your navel
And the deep forest darkness of your crotch
Where there is all beginning and all end,

Then it may well have strayed northward
To run the long smooth glide that is your neck,
Or thinking of a cool dream lost in sleep,
Slipped under that long hammock of your hair.

ALONE IN THE HOUSE

The house has an air of being half suspended
In peace and nervous waiting. Peace that conceals
The stabbing baby cries, the clatter of children's feet
On the stairs, rising, falling crescendo of quarrels
In the kitchen (and something that the house can't conceal
From itself or anyone for very long), how lonely it is
Without all the bedlam of a family living, growing
Within its four walls.

Now we are all alone in here, no eyes on us,
No-one to say what we shall do or not do,
Alone with our love and the strength that shouts from our
    bodies,
Urging neither haste nor caution. Saying only: these are
    your hours.

29

THE MAGNET

Quite suddenly you rose
From the bench we'd been sitting on,
Moved slowly but steadily away.

I watched your blue coat mix
With the gayer, lighter colours of the crowd.

Then you stopped, hesitated, half-turned
To flash a quick, questioning glance,
Swung your neck, long black hair around again,
Moving on more slowly than before.

It was then my bewilderment, the sense
Of everything crumbling, building and crumbling again,
Melted, and there was only that dull aching emptiness
In the pit of my stomach that cried "You," that shouted "You,"

And I too rose from that bench on the boardwalk,
To follow you, feeling the unfaltering firm magnet
That is our love beginning already to draw us
Tightly, lovingly together once more.

"ONLY A GRAND FOOL SUCH AS I"

Only a grand fool such as I could have forgotten
Your name last night before friends—the name of you
Who has made this dark year glow with the brilliance of
    the sun,
You who have taught me such tenderness, given me such
    strength
To turn in the face of the whole world's scorn, its pitiful dying.

O even the great fool that is me
Will never forget (how could it ever be so?)
The substance that is you, the wit, the laughter, the times
    good and bad with you,
Those thousand little ways of yours, that body I have held
    and loved and known
As intimately as God's touch in the darkness.

O fool to be ever forgetting for a breath's lifetime
Anything that is you, dear, precious, wonderful you!

31

AUTUMNAL

Like the far-blazing forests of maple that burn and burn
    before my eyes
Is the slightest of your smiles when you are happy and no
    sadness lies
Under the dark hair in the slender head. But like the brown
    wet leaves strewn on the ground after rain
Is my heart when in your face there is only dark doubt,
    darker pain.

ON THE UPLANDS

We left the riverbank, the water
Cool-brown and loud with the splashes
Of two small boys with their fat little buttocks
Showing as they dived, and we climbed
The steep hill clinging to the roots
Of old trees, then stood breathless
At the top a long minute before going down
Along the path beside the peaceful fields.

And it was coming back, the dark falling fast,
With the red of the western sun only a memory,
That we stopped beside a tree where a fire
Still glowed from a single log: and soon had it flaming
In a desperate hurry, then threw on grass
To make a smoke we hoped the mosquitoes would choke on,

Because all of a sudden there was so much loving
Bursting in our bodies that everything else was forgotten,
Only me kneeling over you and your body like a flower
Opening to greet the warm sun of my morning.

"THE PROUD ARCH OF YOUR BEAUTY"

There is the perfect curving
Roundness of your breasts, like two gentle
Worlds of wonder, and I cannot forget

The delicate hills and valleys of your neck,
The way your hips hint of waterfalls
Flowing from your waist's hidden springs.

But all these are forgotten, fade into shadow,
When the hands that never tire of meeting your body
Again and again as if for the first time falter

Over the yielding promise of your flanks,
The proud arch of your beauty, O shaped like no thing
    fashioned by man
In all these dwindling centuries of his decline.

33

DON VALLEY AUTUMN

Dark in the valley. Somewhere the noise of water
Running on like forever, hidden, close, menacing.

And the path dips and turns, with me a blind man
In all this darkness, a lost, stumbling creature
Following only the sound of your footsteps up ahead.

Then suddenly I feel the touch of your hand in mine,
Warmly but firmly, and I'm no longer lost
Or alone, in your palm your heart beating,
Life flowing from you to me, the divine spark
Of your love striving to light all darkness, loneliness.

And this night is good.

TELEPHONE RINGING

Downstairs the telephone rang,
And I started up on my bed
Wondering if it could be you.

Opening the door of my room an inch I listened
As the telephone was answered,
Waiting, hanging unbearably off balance.

But no, it wasn't you.
And I lay down on my bed again,
And heard, louder than the warm summer air beating the trees
    outside,
The unnatural hammer-strokes of my heart
Crashing out their loud, diminishing disappointment.

THROUGH THE SHORT TUNNEL

Through the short tunnel that curves
Between the bondage of your dress
And the soft milkweeds of your throat,
My fingers slip, trembling and warm,
Then slowly climb the sudden sloping foothills
Of your breasts, leaving the level plain,
And moving to its crest fondle the two
Bold stabbing nipples of your maidenhood
Waiting so long. Which now, all waiting over,
Rise up to meet the challenge of my love.

ALL THE LEAVES OFF THE TREES

All the leaves off the trees, darling,
Rain grinding them under;
All the flowers dead now, darling,
Only the withered stalks left standing.

Now we shall, lying together,
Remember the long nights and days of summer,
Our summer warm yet, precious yet, intimate as touch,
And autumn, winter shall pass over us
Like the crooked tongues of war that still thunder in our ears.

"WHEN I LOOK AT THE COLD COLD WHITENESS OF THE SNOW"

When I look at the cold cold whiteness of the snow,
I think of the colour of your waist or your thighs
And their snowy whiteness, smooth creaminess,
Under my hand, white, white against my hand.

But there is neither cold nor winter there,
Only the whiteness; all the rest is June
And hot nights dying with no breath of cool,
And mornings waking with the touch of sun.

IN A WINTER

In a winter deep with snow and the feel of death,
There is only you with your smile of summer to keep
The drifts from closing over and the numbing cold
From sinking its iron claws to the roots of my being.

O sick of talk that is only the babble of idiots,
And sicker still of faces and looks of hate,
Of stupid blindness and greed, I lie at your side
And a green world springs from your voice,
Opens bud-like in your hands.

EVENING

No lust tonight in my body, I lie simply beside you
On this bed, and your nearness is enough, the warm soundless
    sigh
Of your breathing is enough, is all for me.
And words we do not speak walk in our heads, are like hands
    touching,
Lips meeting. And over us, gently hovering with the slight
    rustle of his wings,
Sleep is waiting patiently, lovingly, to lead us by the hand
Into the green cool valley of his kingdom.

THE RING

It rests on your finger like a thing come finally home,
And in its sparkle I see
The shining diamonds of our years
Laden down with lustre.

O like a promise, a gleaming talisman,
It holds to your hand, and I could cry easily
Like a little child, being so happy,
But it is so much more fitting to match your smile.

I AM WRITING POEMS

I am writing poems about your beautiful body
While men are working and planning how best to destroy it.
While fiends and madmen arrange our glorious deaths
I am writing poems to sing of the wonders of living;
I am drunk with being alive. I run my hands over your body
While that flesh is still warm and soft and pink,
Not burned or twisted by the faceless men of death
Who are everywhere in this world gone mad, everywhere
In this beautiful, mad, wonderful, death-loving world.

IN THE WHITE TUB

The sweat of our loving together
Glistens and runs on our bodies bending
In the white tub: you bringing the water
In your cupped hand to let it run between
Your two shy breasts, while I want its coolness
On my face and through my hair. And as naturally
As two young children or two fallow deer we clean our bodies,
Pausing only to look up at each other with our love
That shows too deeply now in our eyes and on our lips
For any water to wash away or death to touch,
The years to fade.

AT YOUR BREAST

I am not a child,
But I can suck at your nipples
Not for their milk,
But for the warm peace of them.

And you—
You look down at me
With my mouth worshipping at your breast,
Smiling almost ironically
With the wise knowing of women
At one with their men,
At one with the world.

THE SOURCE

Coming in from a night colder than the eyes of death,
I run to meet your body whose warmth wraps and folds me
In heat flowing in, through and up,
I nuzzle my cold nose on the hot grate of your cheek,
I rub my hands on the furnace of your thighs.

O you are summer-born and breathing heavily
Its sultry breezes of love, you are the heat-waves
Looming up like whirling mirages, and I the doomed swimmer
Struggling helplessly on their crests.

"AS MANY WAYS AS THEY HAVE
TO SAY WONDERFUL"

As many ways as they have to say wonderful
I could talk about you (but why should I bother
To tell them anything?), they never helped me find you,
And sometimes I think they did all they could
To hurt us and kill what we carry in our hearts.

But then I feel sorry for the whole stupid lot of them,
Trapped in their dirty, rotten little lives,
And suddenly I want to give them a glimpse of heaven,
So I write a poem with you lying in a room,
Let them come to its window, look in for a moment at your
    loveliness.

SURPRISED

Naked to the waist like a native girl of Bali,
And gleaming with soap-foam, you are suddenly surprised
In the midst of your bath, and laughingly allow me to kiss
The tip of each breast for the price of a mouthful of suds.

But then I pay you back in the very next moment
When I seek out your mouth and break a bubble or two
In our soft, moist encounter with mint-toothpaste tingle
And no hint at all of foamy, tongue-bitter soap.

LYING BESIDE YOU

Lying beside you, the warm flowing curve of your body
Caresses, encounters the milk-soft thoughts of my love,
And sends them all back to enfold every curve of your body
With the breath of a furnace, the fluttering heart of a dove.

41

MOMENT

See, my little girl-wife rising
From our bed, her breasts nodding
Like a child asleep in a chair,
Her shy flanks moving in rhythm
With the slender waist,
The legs that touch like velvet.

And in a rustle she is gone from the room,
And no poetry of mine or any other
Can bring alive her charm or catch this moment,
Only she can make it timeless, magical.

"I WANT TO THANK GOD"

I want to thank God for the miracle of her body;
For her lips that are never weary of touching my lips
For her lips that never tire of touching mine
With strength and with fire; for her breasts that my hands
    have moulded
In the thousand shapes of my mind and my pleasure;
For her thighs that let flow all the pain in my head and my
    heart;
For her legs that are limpid like water, binding like steel.

O I want to thank God for this beauty that He has showered
So richly, so suddenly on my proud, lonely life,
I want to kneel before her body, give thanks
For this great warmth of summer that is mine after all the
    wind and the snow.

IN WINTER

Snow is alien to me,
Its wolf-pack winds
Light no spark in my blood,
I can only wish them gone
Along with all death-heavy chill.

Then let summer come,
Let the winds be warm
And the nights long
In the bed we lie on,
With snow, wind and chill
As distant as the grave!

O let the nights be long!

THE BROWN AND THE WHITE

My body grows brown beneath the sun.
I feel its fingers kneading at my flesh,
Then sinking down through all my pores
Till each one is an island drowning
In a rising ocean of sweat.

Now when we lie in bed,
Only my buttocks' whiteness
Matches your body's lily,
And I, bending over you in the curve of love,
Am like a dark shadow clouding the sun
For one throbbing, breath-stopping moment.

43

"THE WORLD REVOLVES ABOUT YOU"

The world revolves about you and is you,
By day, by night, in waking or in sleep,
Is soft and gentle as your body turning
Achingly into mine, or muttering and dark
As when a shadow clouds across your mind,
And will not pass until your anger's spent.

O but the world has not the love you have
For me and I for you, it stands
A little to one side, and is ashamed
That two so lowly could become as sun
And moon and all the stars, and looking down
Upon us shakes its head and turns away.

44

NUDE

From looking out at the too-grey folds of rain
Streaking the windows with their spurts, their floods of gloom,
I turn and see your body naked now,
Its whiteness glowing and lighting up the room.

Under the belly's slope the curled black hair,
The breasts small and pointed, the legs tender
As a deer in High Park, O all of it so full
Of a tenderness, a joy, a breathless wonder,

That there is no more rain or darkness falling,
But only the voices of warmth and desire calling.

45

"THIS BED BECOMES OUR ISLAND AND OUR LOVE"

This bed becomes our island and our love,
Tender at first, becomes a savage thing
That swells and grows and suddenly explodes
In wild deliriums of ecstasy.
Then we are strangely quiet, crossing back
To earth again. Our bodies yearn to drown themselves
In water, and our mouths are pierced
And sore with the deep bruising of our lips;
That roused look in your eyes
Calm now, while your body still and loose
Cups into mine and we rest easily.
Now one, now two, but always finally one.

I WANT THE WORLD

I want the world to be as beautiful
As your face and your slender body,
Delicate and warm
As your fingers held out to mine,
O I want all men to be as happy
As the two of us lying together in summer sunshine
Or curled in our bed of winter,
Kind and forgiving as our two hearts touching,
Happy with so little as we are happy,
All eyes turned toward the sun, blazing with our future.

46

Sequence for Susi
1986-1987

A PAIR OF DOVES ALWAYS NEST

A pair of doves always nest
on the smooth ledge of your waist,
hummingbirds always seem
to be arriving and departing
through that trap-door opening and closing
between the lilies of your thighs.

And one thoughtless, quarreling crow
always seems to circle
above your head, as if he wished
with all his dark, evil soul
to be allowed to touch down,
perhaps on your shoulder's welcoming runway
where he'll feel the warm, soft healing of your hands.

YOUR FATHER ALWAYS CALLED YOU DOLLY

Your father always called you Dolly,
because, I suppose, you were small and so fragile
in body at least, and I'm sure those eyes of yours
looking up into his as he held you on his knee
melted all the roughness in him, made him for the moment
a real soft pussy-cat. Like the day he took you by the hand
and said, "Come on, Dolly, all the money I have is the
    fifty cents
in my pocket, so what can I do with that?
Let's you and me go to the movies. . . ."

48

PREDICTION

You look under fifty,
I feel at least seventy.

If we must have each other
so often, so completely,
I predict by the end of the year
we'll be even more years apart!

MINOR MIRACLE

What if that taxi had stopped
in answer to my wave,
would we still be together today?

I don't want to think about it,
rather give a silent prayer
to God and the Fates
that it didn't—that we are!

49

BEGINNING TO WRITE THIS

Beginning to write this I marvel
for perhaps the first real time how little
the years have changed you, those lonely, desolate years
that the world has known and we have known.
Yes, your hair is now a lighter shade, the lines have come
even to your face, though they've been unable
to have their way with a skin tied deeply
to Sicilian beauties. As for your body,
it now has tricks and moves when pressed against mine
that it never had before, which sends my glib words
scattering up into the air like worthless sand!

But O my beauty, what the years have done to me
with my code of not caring, self-indulgence, worthless whims
is not pretty to see or even stomach,
and now I've reached those hours when I panic,
I flounder in dark water on a graveyard sea,
and only the distant, steady lighthouse flash
of your constant presence offers any hope for me.
Please, I beg you, still point the way to shore,
however dimly, or I drown.

IN OLD NEW YORK

Beneath our hotel-room window
it seemed every bus
on Fifth Avenue turned.

But we heard little
of that endless gear-grinding,
making love till we fell asleep
in each other's arms!

THAT BENCH AFTER FORTY YEARS

That bench on the side of the hill
is still there. I walked above it
in the park today,
looked down and there it was,
our secret shelter of forty years ago
still very much the same, though no doubt worn
even smoother from new generations of lovers'
clothes, bodies rubbed along its length
in playful movements, passionate slidings,
and deeply cut, pock-marked by even more
crude hearts, rough initials carved
for all who come after to smile and wonder at.

And the same trees seem to bend
their most discreet, leaf-laden branches
as far down in the same way
we found them that night in our first year together,
as if wanting to still keep our love their secret
or hoping at least that we'd some day return . . . .

OUR HOUSE

I see now my world begins
at the back door, ends at the front;
your face and form in every room
is the reason for my life,
its light, its sustenance.

I live or die here.

THIS AUGUST

How do we know it's August?
One way is because when we step out
every day now on our back-yard lawn,
our feet crush with a silent squish
half a dozen berries hidden in the grass
from our gnarled flowering crabapple tree:

which for us is only one more of a hundred
daily unimporant things we've learned to share,
but which have magically become
each a joyous signpost
of our new-found lives together.

HOLDING HANDS IN BED

If the fingers of your hand
now so warmly, lovingly nestling mine,
could become my private abacus, why, I'd have to count
all the long way to forty
to spell off all the years again.

YOUR LIPS THAT CAN DIG

Your lips that can dig like shovels
or brush against mine so lightly
the image is born in a second
of two butterflies colliding—

at this very moment hover
beside me so tantalizingly close,
I'm dreaming again of hummingbirds
on miniature wings beating up a whispering storm
as they buzz upward, dart downward and sideways,
undecided now which loving part of the flower
to kiss next: so your lips wait near mine.

PLAIN FACT

My arms have never
been clever enough, wise enough
to know how to grab off
half your love for me.

GODCHILD OF THE WESTERN WIND

Deep-baying, desolate was the sound
the swirling Prairie winds of Alberta made
as they swerved around the corners of your house at night,
as they followed you out in the early-morning light
to the ice-cold privy at the back of the frozen yard,
as they roared up behind you as you rode bravely along,
tiny girl on a giant old creature of a horse
on the way to school and back, as they pawed at the windows
as you sat in the two-room schoolhouse and tried to listen
to the teacher at the front of the class. That wind even
    mocked you then
as it rolled along the roof, even moaned like a dying thing
down the shivering chimney; then all the long way home
    again
on your shuffling mare as it blew and blew and blew
the two of you along like leaves, or so it seemed then
to a ten-year-old girl, godchild of the western wind.

YOUR HAIR ONCE COALHURST BLACK

Your hair once Coalhurst black
now York City's golden-brown.
Bastard time we can't disown
or force his smug clocks back.

MY CARIBANA QUEEN

Always you are my Caribana week,
my festival of summer. Every time you smile
it's as if the shiniest morning of July
was lighting up the sky and every cloud
a full-rigged schooner sailing down the wind,
a sun of gold blazing blessings on us all.

That's when I want the most to lift you up
on the highest float in the parade, and say to all:
"Look, there's my darling, Queen of the Carnival,
wave to her, pay her homage, treasure her
as I always hope to treasure her while she walks
beside me on this earth, draws breath
in unison with mine."

YOUR IMPORTANCE TO ME

You push the intoxicating air out through my nostrils,
you pump the life-quickening blood through each coursing
    vein.
So don't you see that your last breath will also be mine,
that with your last surge of blood I cross the river with you?

I SHALL FEEL DEATH

I shall feel death already nudging me
from the first moment I no longer hear
close to my side the steady breath-strokes
of your body echoing mine,

with its breathing in, "Live,"
its breathing out, "Never die."

A very clever machine the body,
at times much too smart for itself,
especially when it thinks itself God
and so will last forever.

56

BONUS

Each day longer with you is a bonus,
a dividend never previously declared,
a zephyr wind of spring and warmth of summer
to fight the tree-stripped autumn desolation,
winter's grinning, snow-ice skeleton.

YOUR DRUGSTORE COWBOY

Something suddenly clicked on, then kicked out inside me,
like a young steer kicking up its heels in mad abandon
at a wild-west rodeo show—the sight of your profile
of exquisite nose, dancing eyes, rose-petal lips,
blending with all that black, flowing hair
across the room from me (room in which every noise
had been squeezed out of it like a sponge,
even the slightest whisper) . . .

And there I was, your drugstore cowboy
from far-off West Toronto,
hopelessly caught in the slick lassoo
your eyes had snapped once, then twice at me,
twin spinning lariats throwing this buckaroo
for his first fatal fall,
which he even welcomed now, wouldn't change for the world,
beginning of a dream fulfilled
he hoped would last forever.

SHORT SHORT SONG

When Susi smiles I'm happy,
when Susi's sad I'm sad.
So as long as we're together
let the whole world go mad!

LIKE YOUR OWN TRUE KNIGHT

Like your own true knight riding proudly out,
black armour shining in the sun, white charger breathing
winter smoke from his nostrils,
I leave this castle behind, you and all within it
so precious to me, and face the hostile world
beyond the next hill and the next, knowing only
that I'm armed with your shield of fidelity and honour,
your splendid sword of hope and compassion,
surely more than enough to tide me through
my deepest trials, sorest temptations.

And as sure as I know the sun must rise tomorrow,
I'll come riding back almost before you know I've gone,
with my mission accomplished, with my one only thought
to doff this intolerable armour, take you in my arms
as crushingly, as lovingly, as any knight of old.

BUTTERCUP

Buttercup underneath your chin—
it's not the yellow of the sun
that shines there, but our love
still gleaming with a stubborn,
almost inexplicable glow!

59

TWO PIGEONS ON THE ROOF

In one quick glance
spotted two plump pigeons on the low-sloping roof
of the Casa do Mosto, saw them huddled close together,
feathers touching, beaks lovingly pecking one another.
You and me, I thought at once,
seeking shelter in each other from the storms of autumn
and the whole frigid, shivering earth, content to spend
the coming ice-sheathed winter
under the Arctic deep-freeze of the underpass
as long as we are one, facing even worse if we have to,
and nothing, not even death,
can shake us or break us . . . .

Lady of the short wings,
delicately ribbed, daintily webbed.
Gentleman of the splendid plumage
posing slightly with uncertain fluttering,
both of us feel now warmth rising all around
as our love glows between us like a blessed presence,
sure, very patient, breathing softly, "Forever."

THANKS TO YOUR LOVE

My heaven-pointed rocket
bursting deep inside of you
as if for the very first time!

Star-scraped, our moon-shot arcs;
breathless, we drift
slowly back to earth again.

THREE WORDS OF A LIE

"I love you"—
three words of a lie
I used for almost forty years,
first on a beautiful, long-haired bride,
then continued on a patient, caring
even more beautiful woman,
who remained at my side
when my only loves were myself
and the white stallion I rode
so hard my spurs cut her,
that old bitch Poetry . . . .

Now when I wish to use the words,
meaning them straight from the heart,

deeper still from the gut of me:
"You're my one guiding light,
without you I'm dead bones,
a turned-off brain, a bewildered nothing,"

even my own mouth mocks me,
makes word-echoes that repeat
and won't stop or leave off:
"Here's that unabashed,
bare-faced liar again,
with words that only spell out
more deceit, endless falsehoods,
so once again be warned,
believe them, one or all,
at your most certain peril."

ALMOST AS HIGH A CHARGE

Almost as high a charge
is now the uncoupling, sweet, slow joy
of separating leg from leg,
then warm, sweating thigh from thigh,
belly from love-touching belly,
one slowly becoming two,
somehow separate again,
close beside the other lying,
breath regular at last,
back on staid earth once more.

But promising to leave this wobbly planet
on an early flight, taking off in a burst of fire,
our space-ship aimed at now-familiar moon and stars.

RIDING THE OLD HORSE INTO DIAMOND CITY

I can see that I'm frustrating you
almost as much as that day in your early childhood
when you tried to ride the old tired horse
into Diamond City for some kerosene
to start the house lamps up again,
but never got there, that ancient animal
(much like me) insisting on taking you
against your will in the opposite direction,
so that you ended up coming home crying,
wondering what made him so stubborn,
and why couldn't things
go a little easier sometimes
even in an upside-down world?

DECLARATION

Although I've already got it written
in the largest of squeaky chalk capitals
on the freshly brushed blackboard of my heart,

some night I'm going to gather all my guts together,
take my paint spraygun down to a certain large city wall,
and by some miracle will have no trouble at all
with what my brain is telling my hands to do
as I work away in the bat-dark shadows.

Then, in the dawn, the first subway passengers
riding east for the short two hundred yards
of the open cut west of Keele station will see
so plain on that impossible-to-miss, familiar showcase
of a hundred love-messages a fresh one staring out
in gleaming-bright colours at least two feet high:
RAYMOND LOVES ROSALIA FOREVER & FOREVER

and no doubt some riders will still be shaking their heads
at the show-off antics of young lovers
as their train moves on through the early-morning light.

63

SLEEPY, SHADOWY TOWNS

Redcliff, Diamond City,
Commerce, Shaughnessy,

sleepy, shadowy towns
of your lost Alberta,

which today have no reason for being
except that you once walked their streets,
breathed their air, took shelter
within their brief boundaries.

IN THE FIRST HOUR OF THIS NIGHT

In the first hour of this night
I shall sing of your love,
which, while it wasn't there at first,
began to grow slowly like a wildflower seed
which finds itself planted by the winds of chance
in a strange, forbidding garden. Then gradually begins
to come alive, as first some sunshine breaks through
to its shady corner, then life-restoring rain drips down
from leaves of giant trees above; and something stirs
patiently inside it, waiting.
Then one day it feels itself swelling
along all its modest length as a bud pushes through the stem,
and then so gloriously swift appears a first flower.

That's the way, wasn't it, that your love for me
bloomed in its first, most unexpected hour!

64

SOME NIGHTS

And then there are some nights
when you lie close beside me
(you fast asleep, me awake),

when the gentle wave-stroke of your breathing
is the only thing left to convince me
I am still alive.

WHEN THE DAY OF THE CORN ROAST CAME

You shouldn't have been too surprised
when the day of the corn roast came,
and you found out along with all our friends
of the Friday-night feast in the Don Valley woods,
that I hadn't bought a single cob of corn,
not one package of weiners, let alone buns,
no jars of mustard, even soft drinks or marshmallows.

You should have known then or at any rate guessed
that my mind was a thousand miles away from food and drink,
that all I wanted was to get you out there alone
among the dark shadows of a friendly tree,
kiss hell out of your full, delicious lips!

BEFORE YOU'RE AWAKE

I'm awake in a silent house
without a whisper in any room.
I imagine even the low scratch
of my pen on paper
may somehow be amplified and reach
the bedroom where your head centres
the pillow's rectangle. That and the scrape
the brush in my hand made earlier
brushing our cat's purring fur.

Now the whole morning waits with me
for your first stirring noises, creak of our bed
as your feet touch the floor two rooms away,
so that another day may be officially unveiled
and yield up its surprises,
with your bowl of oatmeal finished
and a cup of tea raised to your lips—
at which time I'll return your salute
with my first joyful cup of coffee.

66

IN THE SECOND HOUR OF THIS NIGHT

In the second hour of this night
I shall sing of your tenderness
so often like the touch of your fingers
vibrating in these outposts of my body
come alive and singing endless songs of you:

but which at other times can pass me right by
with its perfect naturalness. I don't know I've been trans-
    formed
and made whole again, being so distant, so uncaring
in my ignorant way that I haven't an inkling
that you've moved right inside me,
are working your own delightful magic,
sure sign of your love that I in my blindness
of stubborn heart and mind can't even acknowledge.

Yet even all this hasn't stopped you through the years
when it could have, should have. You've gone undaunted
along in your own quiet, uncomplaining way,
kept reaching out with this great, marvelous gift
of your heart's tenderness to me,
the loved but so-insensitive one.

IF I SHOULD BE THE FIRST ONE CHOSEN

If I should be the first one chosen
to sever our partnership, take the long voyage all alone
to the other side, rest assured, darling,
that within a week or two
(or sooner if I can arrange it),
you'll hear a familiar noise at your door
of a cat meowing, and when you open it up,
you'll see (if I'm granted my wish) a little kitten clawing
to get inside (carbon copy of our own precious Bonnie),
and stooping down you'll pick up a trembling bundle
of pulsing, frantic feline, know at the same instant I do
we're back again in each other's loving arms!

68

THE THIRTIETH OF NOVEMBER

As the morning sun melting at this very moment
the first, faint frost-breaths of winter
out there among the mounds of still-surviving leaves,

so our love may falter, buffeted in turn
by the iron fists of winter, then warmed uneasily
by capricious late-November sunshine: and so we must take
    heart,
think always spring gazing out into the ruins
of our garden, look far beyond this life-in-death
of the sodden moment. For the seed will only allow itself
to lie barren the length of the winter's whim,
the sap's only waiting on hold
to spring up again through the branches
of these calvarine trees. So, too, our love will be reborn,
flow again through our veins like electric, life-giving fire!

OF SUCH SIMPLE THINGS

About to put the car in reverse,
backing out of our awkward driveway,
I caught sight of you in the back yard
not more than twenty feet away,
entirely oblivious, it seemed, to all else in the world
but the grey squirrel you were trying your hardest
to coax down from a branch of our crabapple tree
and take the piece of biscuit from your tempting fingers.

Such a wonderful brief moment!
The almost angelic look on your face,
the bobbed bushy tail that was the squirrel
hanging upside-down from the tree—

Of such simple things
are love and sweet contentment made.

70

THE CHINOOK OF YOU

There are hours when my world can be endless winter
rimmed round with treacherous ice, deep-frozen through,
lifeless, harder than the highest icicle,
but shapeless, blunted, floundering in sleet and snow.

That's when you always seem to flow into a room
that's like a prison to me, sweep right in
with your beauty radiant, body wrapped
in a hundred melting breezes. How the temperature rises
and everything melts and flows again and sings
in my winter world, now transformed and shining,

the chinook of you stealing through the foothills
of my January life, thawing graveyard snows away
in one long breath of warmth and deep compassion.

EARLY

I'm up before the opening
of dawn's first rosebud,
just to celebrate the fact of you.

TONIGHT I FEEL THE SAME BELL-RINGING JOY

Tonight I feel the same bell-ringing joy
for you and all you mean to me as I did
that night over forty long years ago,
when I missed the last Runnymede bus
after running all the way from Carrick Avenue
to the Keele-St. Clair terminal.

Missed it by at least three breathless minutes,
so stood for a moment wondering which way
to walk the long hike home—straight along St. Clair
past the late-night putrefaction
of Swift's and Canada Packers, and right across from them
the stockyard's fresh, not-so-fresh dung smells
waiting there to greet me like a long-lost friend,
a still-vivid memory—or perhaps instead cut down Keele
    Street,
where my footfalls would echo and re-echo
all the long cavern journey of the underpass,
and after it a dozen rambling, slumbering streets
with their already-nodded-off houses,
to pass by like a stranger as if for the very first time . . . .

Well, I was in no mood for slaughterhouse vistas,
I remember that so distinctly—I was totally drunk with
  you,
with the very thought, the slightest touch of you,
and I didn't need any distractions—so chose to take Keele
  Street,
then Annette to Runnymede, and all that short half-hour
I could have done cartwheels the whole damn distance
to my Beresford Avenue home, but settled for a carnival
of coloured lights, flashing smiles, all whirling through my
  head,
young man of twenty-five in love like a calf-sick teenager,
bewildering, crazy-happy hours!

And tonight, I swear, it's all back with me again!

CONFESSION

The first time I saw you
to have this lightning thought:

O to be the one that's sheltered
beneath the long dark tent-cloth
of her hair forever!

73

THE RESCUE, AND AFTER

"The supreme test of a marriage comes when one partner is able to snatch the other right out of the jaws of the abyss—the abyss being separation and its attendant loneliness, which is worse than death itself. The only casualty sometimes then becomes the rescuer, who may find the cost of rescue too high a price to pay"—John Edward Fox, Jr.

I

I was slipping off life's precipice,
hands no longer gripping, the abyss
of my vulnerable remaining life
suddenly bottomless, hell-dark. And it was then
that I felt your fingers touching mine
(that so easily could have turned away),
then clutching my hands, slowly pulling me back
inch by inch, to a reprieve. The fingers, hands
of my one, my only true friend, that showed their love
by not abandoning me, by dragging me back
from death into life renewed, a new beginning.

74

2

But in reaching out for me,
in hauling me back from the edge
of that abyss, your eyes had to take
one long look down into that hell,
that soot-black, endless shaft,
and that was enough for the darkness there
to rend your own life, split your soul
and your body straight in two, flood your heart
with the stinging vinegar of hate,
gall and wormwood of living death.

3

While I, saved by a miracle,
not earned or deserved, pulled around me again
my shell of hurt and isolation, shutting you out
at the very moment of your need,
as you cried out for understanding.

75

4

So once again
when you asked the least from me
I could only give you less.

YOUR EYELIDS STIRRING

Your eyelids stirring after sleep

dawn's gentle prying-open
of the day.

76

BELIEVE ME, I'M NOT WAITING

Believe me, I'm not waiting
until Death slips two shoes on your feet
that seem like the perfect fit at last
(no more rubbing at the toes, no weakness in the arch),
so that you find yourself getting up
and walking right out of this life
like a young girl without a care in the world
in her first high heels.

No, I'm not waiting
like Hardy to walk again Beeny Cliff
one year too late. I'm not waiting like Montale
to catalogue in a list of touching remembrance
the mystery that was his dear little Mosca.

No, I'm squeezing down hard
on all the sweet-tasting orange pulp
that is today, leaving the tart
lemon rind of tomorrow for all those
so eager to suck dry
its mouth-puckering bitterness . . . .

I'm seizing the present moment
to celebrate what we have, what we feel,
what we touch together now while our fingers still intertwine,
while our bodies can still come alive,
glow, yes, even sing their strange, unreal, beautiful song!

SPOONS

Before I met you a spoon
was that round, curved piece of metal
very useful to help me eat my cereal,
or to stir the cream in my first
life-saving coffee of the day.

Since then that shiny breakfast tool
has become a symbol of joy as our bodies
form themselves into a spoon-shape
of warmth and contentment. Sometimes I'll be
its outer curve, feel the inner shape of you
fitting itself behind me. Then, turning,
I'm that inside curving
that seeks out your waiting form,
and knees locked behind, feet entwined,
nestles your buttocks' radiant heat
into my loins' slumbering pocket.

That's why the knife and fork
mean so little to us:
but the spoon is something else,
a reminder, if you will, of our times of wonder.

IN THE THIRD HOUR OF THIS NIGHT

In the third hour of this night
I shall sing of the skin of your precious body,
stretched on its bone-frame much like the pulled-tight
    fuselage
of the airplanes of my youth: and like those same aircraft,
whose ride was unpredictable and wild,
you voyage out with me on that white and rosy airframe
covering the wings of your arms, the rudder of your waist,
and all the other fabulous component parts
that make up you. And I think of your father,
worker from the age of eight in Sicilian sulphur mines,
of his rough, bronzed face belying the soft white skin
of his chest and arms; and of your mother, that miniature
    donna,
whose skin had the same soft feel in the arms,
whose face with its flawless, innocent covering
I'm sure almost drove your father mad with desire . . . .

You, goddess, have that very same skin today,
angel-wrap that still makes my desire
overflow at a single touch, one quick stroking!

THIS IS THE MONTH

This is the month the eye cries out for green,
rejects the tattered grey, the unfeeling brown
of winter's ruin. O if we could only
houseclean the dust-filled, well stained heart,
give the soul a good scrubbing-down
along with the scuffed floors, imprisoning walls—

O then we could lean into spring winds blowing,
all the useless rest thankfully disown!

80

MAKING PASTA TOGETHER

Me, who never learned to boil water,
all thumbs where I should be fingers
in any hands-on situation,
tonight find myself an eager novice
in our old-fashioned kitchen
where we'll make the evening meal together
(you already having summoned all the patience,
the grim determination of your stoic
Sicilian grandparents to see you through it . . . .)

First thing, you say, is to collect the utensils
and all the ingredients we'll need. So first out comes
our big aluminum pot, and next let's not forget
the Teflon frying-pan on which we'll place half a kilo
of Armadale Meats' finest ground steak
to stir gently until well browned.

Meanwhile our pot is filled up half-way
with water, to which you personally add a palmful of salt
along with another prayer underneath your breath
for the whole operation. Then we start bringing this
to the quickest boil. And as this is all getting well under way
we're magically simmering on the element opposite
a jar of prepared tomato sauce with mushrooms and spices
in our fancy new shatter-proof glass saucepan;
by the time this starts to bubble gently
the pot of water starts to boil in unison,
and you take a fat measure of our favourite rotini-shaped
       pasta,
plop it in the pot, while to help out I set the timer
for twenty minutes on the nose (just right to allow the pasta
to become *al dente*, which I suppose means

not too soft, not too chewy) : all this time I haven't forgotten
the ground beef now browning beautifully, coaxing it along
with slow, careful stirring. My face feels nearly as well done
as the meat, which you agree is now ready to be added
to the slowly simmering sauce. So I carefully push the meat
    morsels
down the saucepan toboggan-slide into the beautifully red,
bubbly, aromatic liquid. Now that it's well mixed
the two can leisurely caress each other
while the pasta cooks on, and we take a well deserved load
off our feet as all cooks love to do,
sit down in the living-room until the timer
brings us marching back into the kitchen
to complete our joint operation.

Now with one deft movement you transfer the boiling pot
to the sink and the waiting plastic colander: presto,
a thick pile of steaming, glistening rotini's left
as our utensil drains swiftly, and with yet another
lightning flick of the wrist you've transferred it to the
    saucepan
where it sinks in delight well down into the quivering
meat-laden sauce. A few more skilful stirs
and the pasta's well mixed, stares invitingly from the pan.

82

Only one last final touch—grated parmesan cheese freely
    shaken
in three deft relays with the big spoon stirring all the while,
and the steaming pot is ready to be whisked
across to the sideboard where you begin to spoon
the glorious food into two new big plates,
your practical eye making sure we leave
enough for another good meal. What more's left to do
than to move to our table, bring our forks up
for the ritual first bite of the feast, almost always the one
you remember the most afterward as you recall
how your taste-buds came alive and leaped to greet
another pasta celebration, Christmas and New Year's
all rolled together, soul-satisfying, belly-memorable!

STRAWMAN

Anger surging up from my gut,
unreasonable, uncontrollable bile,
mostly when your words strike fire,
go leaping out to catch me unaware,
singe me before my firefighter love
comes welling up to douse the spreading flames,

that love and tenderness
your vulnerable strawman
still holds for you in his secret, inner heart,
my lady.

OLD MONTREAL MATCH-BOOK COVER

(For Audrey)

"The smallest Hole in Town
MARCUS CLIP-JOINT
409 Milton Street
Montreal
Where the Customer is Always Wrong"

one side of the match-book cover reads,
while the flip side says:

"Stale Bread
Sour Milk
Dry Tobacco
Old Magazines
Rancid Butter
Rotten Eggs
Contaminated Groceries
Exorbitant Prices
and Lousy Service

We also Chop Keys
and Butcher Locks."

And today to look it over once, then again,
this battered, grey match-book cover
gathering dust in my desk for almost forty years
right from that morning John Sutherland lit a cigar
with the first match torn from it, then handed it to me,
a small memento of Durocher Street—is to remember what
    days those were—
what scenes, what happenings
break loose now from the log-jam
of abandoned, long-forgotten years,
what faces stare out at us,
some dead, some still among the living,
how they all suddenly come alive,
strut, laugh and scream,
do all those human things
so beautifully once more!

And don't forget, you and I walked those Montreal streets,
sat in rooms, in cafés, with those sparkling people now so
    remote,
the almost unreal strangers of our past: and all of them
in some way left their mark on us,
they and their proud, grim, shoddy, tender city
of the Forties, the Fifties,
touched us deeply, changed us forever.

85

FROM THE FIRST MOMENT I SAW YOU

From the first moment I saw you
across the bedlam of that office room
(me, airman with his wings well clipped,
walking the bumpy tarmac of reality,
you, wild Prairie rose,
transplanted to a hothouse Toronto),

you were my salvation, fresh and unspoiled
as an early spring morning.
This is love, I thought,
feeling my heart do a double roll to port,
I must have this darling creature for my own,
and I set about winning you.

Was I wrong that first day?
Wasn't I right to follow
the impulse making all my five senses reel?

Cool intellect may tell me differently today;
more than forty years have sobered
any recklessness left in my heart.
But that first time I glimpsed you
across that crowded office space,
I was still hopelessly young, an innocent
the world had yet to batter.
Yes, I could only say, yes,
my greedy hands reaching out
to pluck such a rare, virginal flower!

And yes, believe me, darling,
I'd obey that same impulse today!

BEATING THE WEIGHT-GUESSER

Though it actually happened only twice
when I was with you, one could imagine it
being repeated over and over.
All that would be needed
was one of those small amusement fairs
that travel through small towns,
set up shop in a city park
for a three-night or a one-week stand.
That and the familiar weight-guesser,
a fast-talking, wisecracking big mouth
who offers to guess a person's weight
within five pounds or you win a prize
(the real prize being to beat this smart-ass);
then of course we'd need you and your small, slim body
(but deceptively firm) with the greatest pair of legs attached,
and your black hair falling loose about your shoulders
as you step up easily on the low wooden platform,
while the weight-guesser makes a show of looking you over
from every angle with his experienced eye,
gives out with a line of patter while he makes up his mind,
finally comes up with: "Let's say the little lady
is ninety-eight lovely pounds," then backtracks and says
       quickly
"No, let's make that ninety-five," and at that
you smile down at me waiting back at the edge of the crowd,
and I see you step casually onto the scale right beside you,
watch the indicator go quickly past 100,
then slowly level off
at 105 well distributed pounds,
stay pointed at that mark.

And you step down from the platform
to join me again, a large box of chocolates in your hand,
and we wander on slowly through the fair, with me wondering
    how long
the two of us can go on eating with enjoyment
a whole box of candy every other night,
as if this were fall-fair time and we were travelling
from town to town through old Ontario . . . .

CARING AND SHARING

Caring and sharing . . . .
To think that all through
the long blurred years
of our lives together,
I never thought to add
those two simple, plain,
all-important words
to the working vocabulary
of my brain and my heart.

MY WILD ALBERTA ROSE

My wild Alberta rose,
my always-faithful wife,
my one true friend
and close companion,

it seems I've waited
all these lost years just to praise you,
celebrate you,
throwing away with abandon,
wasting recklessly,
what could have been, should have been,
our most precious moments together.

Now, when I fear
it's almost too late,
I'm moved to praise you,
trying desperately to salvage
the one thing left worth plucking
from the pitiful wreckage
of my life and loving.

So, my wild Alberta rose,
summon up all your compassion,
sweep the depth of your understanding,
and please listen patiently
to these words of a fool seeking desperately
for a miracle to let him linger
still in the shadow of your love!

THE FIRST TIME

The first time we're close enough to her
we'll both reach up and scratch out
both the eyes of that black bitch Death!

LOCKED TOGETHER

Locked together in that all-too-brief battle
we can only win, never lose, with your tousled head
on the pillow close to mine, the measured breaths
from your exquisite nostrils themselves enough to cool
the sweat gathering on my forehead,

I find your eyes
telegraphing their shared contentment, hinting further ecstasy
as they bridge the inch between us,
going on to dig behind my brain,
gripping all my roused being in their languid purity,

so that hours later there's still that image etched
of two moons mirrored in a dark brown pool.

90

THANK YOU FOR YOUR NOTE

Thank you for the short, two-page note to me in your clear, unaffected handwriting, which you left on my desk this morning. It struck such an immediate cord, triggered such a spontaneous response in me that I wanted to write your message down in some verses of my own: but here it is two weeks later and the way hasn't been shown to me yet how to set it down properly, so I've decided to settle for this rough draft of a prose poem until something may or may not be given to me, utilizing the main points you stressed so that I can return to it myself again and again to draw renewed strength from its loving, penetrating words:

"You count the *bad* hours, the *bad* days, not noticing the many *good* times. I count the *good* hours, hoping for, willing more. You say the glass is half-empty; I say the glass is half-full. And this is very uncharacteristic of you—you who always plunge into things so optimistically, working only toward your goal!

"In this present matter, *the most important of your life*, you are going into it always expecting the worst, almost willing it to go wrong, doing things deliberately to mess up. Haven't you made enough mistakes? You seem to have handled things all your life only to try to make it more miserable. Now you've made your bed but you seem surprised it has thorns in it, and never cease complaining. Don't you want to be happy, or at least content? Why don't you work at it? Please, for the sake of both our lives!"

A CONFESSION TO SUSI

All through the marriage ceremony
I could hear her sniggering faintly
from the next room, even though
she'd never been invited,
and as far as I knew
didn't have my parents' address.

But, while it was distracting and rude,
I couldn't do much about it;
you see, I'd been more than willing
to bring my mistress,
my demanding mistress of Poetry,
into the marriage without you,
my beautiful bride,
being any the wiser . . . .

AT THE FUN-FAIR

Strange that this remains the clearest memory
of our year of courtship together: that night at the travelling
  fun-fair
in Earlscourt Park, where we strolled among the swirling rides
and the frantic cries of barkers, and I never once suggested
we try out the Whip or the ferris-wheel,
both looking like good, innocent fun, or coaxed you into
  tossing
certain small wooden balls at a row of stubby duck pins
to win the grand prize of a cuddly panda doll.
Instead, it was you coaxing me, at first gently,
then almost angrily, to loosen up a little,
spend a quarter on one of the games of chance,
and puzzled that the more you tried
the more stubborn I became.

Strange indeed, but when you re-live that incident of long ago
(too often now for me not to realize
how much I must have hurt you then),
I still can't understand my stubbornness that evening
any more than I can the other hundred and one different
  times
since that night at the fun-fair
when I've behaved like the same childish, up-tight fugitive
from your love and your life, still lost among the ferris-wheel,
the screaming rides, the coaxing shouts of the barkers . . . .

APRIL FOOL

*"April Fool's past
and you're the biggest fool at last."*

On that day all tomfoolery
must be over by noon,
or as the rhyme says
it'll turn back on you.

My April Fool's deception
didn't show its stupid head
until seven hours after,
if I remember correctly,

and this April fool
stood there in front of you
watching his foolish dagger
(no playful, rubber-bladed thing)
sink deeper, deeper into your heart,

without any love or compassion
crossing his idiot jester's face
as your life's blood streamed out in front of him.

SMALL-TOWN GIRL

Shaughnessy, Commerce,
Redcliff, Diamond City,
even Coalhurst belongs in there somewhere,
and I know the order isn't chronological
with your life, only with the brain I have—
you could tell me the story today
of each of those small Alberta towns,
all you can remember of them, and by tomorrow
I'd have them all hopelessly scrambled
as only I can mix things up good and proper.

But when all's said and done, how important is it
whether the roof blew off your four-room house
in Redcliff or Shaughnessy, whether your cat Blackie
had her third litter in Commerce or Diamond City,
or if you crawled through the heat-ducts in the school
at Coalhurst or wherever? For me, anyway, it's each event
in your life that I treasure
almost as much as you treasure them yourself,
not the time or the place of them;
the insights, the clues from the past
that I've slowly gathered of your life,
all a necessary part of the understanding
of you as a person, a living, breathing human being.

So now that I'm desperately trying
to sort out every lost event, each fleeting impression
that I've retained of you, I can only do it
in my own worst, mixed-up way,
which means I can only hope for your understanding,
your forgiveness as I grope among the shadows,
the scattered fences of your Prairie childhood.

THE BLACK-WIDOW SPIDER

Let's say that you were twelve
that morning at recess
in your Shaughnessy school,

when an older boy pointed down
into a narrow mine-crack
at one end of the yard,

and with a small stick poked
at the gleaming, coal-black shell
of the widow spider, flipped her over

so you saw the distinct
red marking on her belly,
knew right away with a shiver

this was the deadly,
very poisonous black widow
so helpless before you,

96

but had to leave it there
as your teacher came out then
loudly ringing his bell

that told each boy and girl
morning play-time was over,
and back into the schoolroom

you marched, already thinking
of the classes ahead,
not realizing

you'd added one more picture
to your growing collection
of a strange, outside world.

97

DREAM WITH CHARGING ANIMAL

"The animal that charged you like a bull
in your dream—did he have flaring nostrils?"

"Not that I remember. The one detail I've kept
is that of a narrow, weasel-like face
with menacing eyes that seemed to shine and reach out
like miniature headlights as he came at me."

"Then it couldn't have been a bull,
I can't imagine one looking at all like a weasel."

"Well, it might have been even a man's face—
perhaps even the devil himself
come to claim a new disciple."

"By the way you jumped in the bed,
flailed your arms about, kicked out with your legs,
I'm sure you would have scared off
even the devil for good."

"They say he doesn't give up that easy;
but if by any chance it was him
let's hope it did.
That was one bad dream too many."

"And besides, our bed
won't stand much more strain like that."

TO MY BUS-DRIVER

(8 AM Kingston-Toronto Express)

Mr. Voyageur-Colonial, why don't you clear
the whole damn passing-lane of this Queen's Highway
all the way to TO by giving out
one blast to end all blasts on your matchless horn?
And then why can't you jack up your cruising speed
from 90 km to 290, earn the pole position
at next year's Indianapolis? Don't you know
I've got a helicopter waiting with blades whirling,
right on the top of the Scarborough Town Centre,
so eager to sweep me over the city smog
in one smooth transporting blur
to my back-yard landing-strip,
where my Susi waits for me, two tulips from our garden
in each waving hand as red-glowing markers
to guide me safely down to the glide-path
of her welcoming arms . . . .

Mr. Voyageur-Colonial, put your foot right down
to the floor, show your backside
to every hot-shot trucker—

please hurry, get me home!

IF THE BIRDS

If the birds
can sing themselves hoarse this morning,
then so can I.

For my life's a thousand times more blessed
than any of theirs, I'm sure.

Sing myself hoarse,
soaked by the warm spring rain falling,
while I'm lifted up, sent sailing down the wind
on the wings of your tireless caring!

SWEET-AND-SOUR CHICKEN BALLS

Our lives so far
sweet-and-sour chicken balls.

The sourness in me
delicately counterbalanced
by the sweetness in you.

What a most delicious
unexpected blending
we make together!

FORTY-YEAR RING

The wedding-ring that once
slipped off your finger so easily,

and even after many years
yielded to soap or Vaseline,

now is stubbornly wedged there,
and as we watch the jeweller

cut through it quickly
with his sharp, relentless tool,

more than an old ring is being abandoned,
though we can't give it a name,

but there's no sadness here today
as we cross to the other side of the store

to look at new rings, one of which
will soon grace your finger

on that special day in June
when our two lives were joined,

our pledge to be renewed
for at least another forty years!

THIS FIRST RAMBLING BUMBLE-BEE

Forced to make a detour
around my propped-up ladder
in the flowerbed under the window,

this first rambling bumble-bee of summer
couldn't help but make my day.

"Just think, mighty human,
if you were in my shoes
you could taste a hundred versions
of her indescribable lips
with only one flower-sweep
of this so-called garden!"

SONG OF A MAN WHOSE HOUSE IS OUT OF ORDER

Make me over, Mystic Mother,
for I badly need (make that *desperately*)
a major renovating. This house that's my heart
has roof leaks, leaf-plugged eaves
oozing with foul muck, sour water,
worn and peeling paint everywhere, even ceilings
cracked, the wallpaper loosening . . . .

How can I expect you,
my lover, my one true friend, to live in such a wreck
of a place with me any longer? God only knows
how you've put up with it all these years
so patiently, so uncomplainingly,
but now it's time to stop, I've got to make
this house my heart a fit dwelling,
or move out of it altogether,
leave it for the wrecker, the wandering junkman . . . .

It's going to take at least a minor miracle,
but miracles do happen; and this house my heart
can still shine in every room, a new spirit
flow through it much like vibrant music playing!

ONLY ONE DAY AWAY FROM YOU

Only one day away from you
(daylight an endless, hateful time
in the midst of sunshine, happy, smiling faces,
night-time an endless, senseless staring
at stubborn clock-hands that refuse to move).

O I'm disoriented, lost,
a wobbly wheel wanting everything to stop,
by which I mean everything, my mixed-up
poet's fantasy of a life perhaps
the best example of all.

If I didn't know
you still cared for me,
still waited to welcome me home,
what would become of me?

Quite simply then
I thank God for the shining
continuing miracle of you.

BACK RUBBING

It's a good thing your skin itches
after taking a bath, otherwise at this very moment
I wouldn't be watching you roll over naked
onto your stomach, then wait for the touch
of my four right-hand fingers
with a dab of body-lotion on each of them,
to start to rub the smooth lowland of your shoulders
with a lover's warmth, then glide gently down
so you're hardly aware of it into even smoother
slough-country where your waist begins almost right away
the imperceptible upward sloping, which my fingers recognize
as a hint of foothills, and are confirmed as first
they climb the steep slippery side
of one buttock, then head due east to meet the other,
a difficult, strange country they linger in,
reluctant to leave for a dozen flesh-kneading reasons;
finally slide off toboggan slopes to touch the thighs, the legs'
    beginnings,
more unusual country again. Now as quickly as possible
those fingers finish their work here,
head back into the foothills: they're looking now
(though they'll not find) the mountains they feel cheated of,
although they have no real reason to—
but what else can you expect of human fingers?

IN MY DREAM

Advancing slowly without a sound
deeper, deeper into that springtime wood,
I came to a sunlit clearing, and there on the grass
you whitely naked lying at your ease.

It seems without a word between us
I joined you there.

HAIRCUT

"I won't mind your hair turning white
when you get old," you once told me,
adding, "just as long as you don't go bald."
These playful words were said, I believe,
the year before we were married.

This morning, forty years later,
I sit in a barber's chair, watch small clumps
of my white hair falling
on the even whiter gown wrapped around me,
figuring I've got another five years
of living and loving with you,
before you'll catch the last white hair that vanishes
from my thick skull, then glowing
like a well polished table-top . . . .

THE SURPRISE

Your kiss when it came
swallow-swift,
caught me unawares,

but I swear I'll be ready,
even waiting the next time
(may it come very soon),

have my tiny net ready
to snare it forever
on the edge of your lips,

so my starved pair waiting
for a long week now
may feel your healing touch.

107

CHILDHOOD WORDS

At age five two words
in your own private language were:
first "medvee," which you conjured up
to describe the sight of the dark-grey silhouette
of a figure in long clothing breasting
the Prairie wind head-on as she strode
across your farm's back border, her clothes and her kerchief
streaming behind her . . . .

Then, after watching your mother sewing by hand,
and noticing the knot she made
at the end of the thread,
something in your head formed the strange word "dugnia,"
and it seemed so right that your Italian mother
used the word herself after that . . . .

Granted, two words never made a language—
but how many of us ever got as far as you
before those first five magic years
were left behind and lost forever?

RIDING OFF TO ROLLING HILLS SCHOOL

Some mornings your father would saddle
the big ageing horse, then lift you up all the way
to your rider's perch, where you watched him
adjust the stirrups, slip your tiny feet in,
finally hand you the two loose reins,

and with a slap from his work-roughened hand
on the rump of the gentle beast,
off the old brown mare would go
down the Prairie road over three miles' worth
of dust, sun and rain
from the farm to the Rolling Hills School.

Barely fifty pounds of girl
with a queasy stomach clinging to the saddle-horn
as you rode off to the two-room schoolhouse . . .
another picture of you from far-away Alberta
that comes alive when I least expect it,
another piece of the shining, shifting mosaic
that is you.

109

SEQUENCE FOR SUSI

(Words for a fortieth wedding anniversary)

I

You, the little farm-girl of five,
being bought one chocolate-bar any Saturday
your father had a nickel to spare,

were smart enough even then
to cut a single piece to eat right away,
then save all the rest in a drawer
for a second piece to savour next day,
and so on through the rest of the week.

While I know very well that I,
city kid of a father
that by some minor miracle
held his job through all the Depression,
would have gobbled the whole bar down
the first minute my teeth got around it!

And hasn't that been
the exact same story
with you and me ever since?

2

After what you've told me
I can almost picture you and your playmate
climbing up that slight Prairie slope, where toward the top
the cactus plants grew, each a small, prickly, grey-green
    mound
with up to three purple flowers bravely pointing upward.

Next, the trick was to find a dried-out flower,
pull it out gently to bring the plump green berry
attached to the end along with it,
ready to surprise your parched mouth
with its sweet honey-nectar.

And have I not caught
in these last few months
a hint of that flavour still on your lips?

3

Small-town girl,
have things changed that much for you
since you saw someone roller-skating
on the street in Lethbridge, coaxed your parents
into letting you have your very own pair;
then, after you'd brought them home, found out
what you should have known all along—
that in Shaughnessy, a village three streets wide
and three streets long, there wasn't one single inch
of hard enough surface to skate on, not even
the dirt road in front of your house.

But you put them on anyway,
tightened them, then stood up carefully,
in roller-skates at last,
a look of defiance on your face
as you looked down, admiring so much it hurt
your beautiful store-bought speedsters . . . .

4

There you were, a delicate windflower,
small perfect bloom of the Prairies
nourished by the wind and the sun,
all under unblemished skies. You'd grown roots
well down into that small-town earth,
and the fates were never more cruel
than the day they uprooted you, brought you here
to Toronto, tried hard to transplant you,
turn you into a hothouse city flower.

But anonymous faces in the street, frantic offices
with busy, scheming thoughts
behind so many pairs of eyes,
could never take the place of those slow, deliberate,
hand-and-heart-touching friendships you'd left behind.

And then the final blow—you meeting me,
and me falling hook, line and sinker for you,
ending up having to possess you. That's when you started
to slowly shrivel the whole length of your stem,
and almost before you knew it the blossom had faded,
and you could have let yourself die quietly . . . .

But to your everlasting credit you denied
all this was happening, fought back in every inner fibre
with your twin gifts of humour and forbearance,
and today that flower of you still blooms,
lives on here in alien soil.

5

In our marriage ceremony
I remember the minister
coming down to the crunch
with his "Love, honour and cherish."
(Did they still ask the bride
to "obey" rather than "cherish"?)

How easy for me to mouth the words
while not holding them in my head.
How frivolously easy
to let those sweet singing birds
flutter out one by one
from the fouled-up birdcage of my mind!

114

6

The day after the wedding
we lunched at the Royal Connaught,
then went to the best picture-palace in town
to see *The Egg and I*, starring Claudette Colbert
and Fred MacMurray, with the first appearance
of Ma and Pa Kettle, which had some funny moments
and put us in good humour,
which I needed very much to be in
after I'd paid the hotel bill, found all I had left
was three lousy dollars and change in my pocket,
along with two return coach tickets
on the Toronto, Hamilton & Buffalo Railway . . . .

But then again who really cared
when I had on my arm the most beautiful and the cleverest
    girl
of all the streetfuls of brains and beauty
to be found in the Queen City of Toronto, Canada!

115

7

Almost right from the day we married,
as soon as all the lights were out
you'd lie flat on top of me
in our new, fancy bed, not to arouse me
but as if to drain away all the fears
and loneliness you'd gathered up all day
alone in our six-room house. And since you were only
ninety-five pounds soaking wet you were light
as a sheet up there (and with many
quite unique advantages), and seeing that our bones
seemed to fit perfectly together,
I'm sure, if I'd been able
to sleep on my back, we'd have spent
(more by accident than anything else)
many whole nights tightly pressed
in each other's arms.

8

Beloved, though this comes
far too late to be of much use,
for what it's worth I see now
(as a blind man suddenly stricken
with the light of a thousand blazing suns),
that your love for me rght from the first day
has been a safety-net caringly erected
without fuss or fanfare to protect me
from the falls that were sure to come,
given my coldness, my indifference
to you or anything else that really mattered.

So, very patiently and without complaint,
you stood close by in your wish
to keep me away from all harm,
your love so strong you could do nothing else
even when all fairness cried out and pleaded
that you forget me, do nothing more.

Then along came that fateful day,
when I in my blindness
threw all caution to the wind,
climbed to the highest tower,
and without a thought of the consequences,
dared that swaying, treacherous wire
that was waiting there to ensnare me,
walked onto it like the fool I was
and sure enough slipped before I'd taken
a half-dozen steps: down I plunged
to be saved from myself
by that strong, loving net of yours
catching me at the very point of death.

And would you believe it,
uncaring, thoughtless fool that I was,
I jumped down from that net,
and without the slightest word
or even silent thanks in my head,
walked off as if nothing had happened,
as if I had never even walked that wire
or slipped and fallen in my arrogance
and been saved when nothing said I should.

Once again that saving net of yours
totally ignored—final blow of indifference
to your patient years of loving.

9

If at any time there's been a hint,
a glimpse of blessed sunlight
at the end of the long, long tunnel,
it's been you and only you
who's opened my poor blinded eyes
long enough to see it,
you, my only guide
to the Promised Land.

10

They say you can't teach
an old dog like me new tricks,
but surely he can work at
beefing up, perfecting
his better ones, giving them
that extra spit and polish,
so they shine daily, even sparkle,
in the eyes of his mistress.

11

People who live forty years together
are either total-crazy in love,
or are bored to tears,
or do so out of convenience,
or are lonely as death,
or haven't got the guts to make a change.

We've tasted every one of these,
have now gone back
to sip at simple love
with all our fingers crossed.

12

Like a nurse in angel-white you led me
out of the dark narrow cell that was my loneliness,
into the green of a morning cooled with dew
freshly scattered, gleaming with the sun's
first burst of praise for a newly minted day.

13

A simple gold band
fitting snugly on my finger,
which I rub lightly
at least once a day

to remind me that this ring
stands for two,
that only half of it
belongs to me.

14

Marvelling at what seems to me
an impossible business—you mending my socks
or sewing up the seat of my pants—
the way you go at it with such loving care
and attention to detail.

I only wish now I could have given
the same attention to your wants,
your needs in years gone by,
and more selfishly—brought to my verses
the same earnest, sober dedication,
I feel as I watch you now,
head bent down closely to your needle,
or your fingers as they guide a garment through
the whirling magic of the sewing-machine.

Work such as this in your hands
becomes the nearest thing to holy.

15

I remember the year we were married
they were still cleaning up the rubble
of ruined buildings in Berlin,
while even then the Hyena and the Jackass
were beginning their open skirmish for that city.

Forty years later they're still at it with hammer and tongs,
both grown to impossible giants, and you and I,
along with the rest of the world,
can only watch from the sidelines
as these two tear each other slowly limb from limb,
with now the world's total destruction
the ultimate prize,
and the only question left unsettled
not why but when.

16

When you are gone
(I'm assuming
that I'll outlive you),
from time to time I'll light
one of the cigarettes you've left,
allow it to burn long enough
for the bitter smoke to fill the room,
then butt it out in the ashtray
with the same careful twist
I must have learned watching you.

17

You and I,
we are one
or we are nothing.

A fact so painfully
self-evident from the start
but one that has proved
the most difficult truth
these years have had to teach me.

123

ISBN 0 88750 680 1 (hardcover)
ISBN 0 88750 682 8 (softcover)

Cover art by Mendelson Joe. Typesetting and design
by Michael Macklem

Printed in Canada

PUBLISHED IN CANADA BY OBERON PRESS